THE WEALTH BLUEPRINT

THE WEALTH BLUEPRINT

Strategies for Financial Freedom

B. VINCENT

QuillQuest Publishers

Contents

Introduction

The Significance of Independence from the Rat Race

Independence from the rat race is something beyond having cash. It's tied in with acquiring the opportunity to pursue life decisions without being excessively worried about the monetary effect. It's tied in with carrying on with your life based on your conditions, getting a charge out of both the present and the future in a fair manner. Accomplishing independence from the rat race implies having an adequate number of reserve funds, ventures, and money available to manage the cost of the way of life you need for you as well as your loved ones. It's tied in with developing your abundance to give you security and genuine serenity.

The excursion towards independence from the rat race begins with grasping its worth. It's not simply an ultimate objective but rather a way to a seriously satisfying, engaged life. With monetary autonomy, you can seek after your interests, face challenges, and invest energy in the things that matter most to you. Whether it's venturing to the far corners of the planet, going into business, or having the adaptability to invest more energy with friends and family, independence from the rat race makes it conceivable.

In any case, for what reason is independence from the rat race so significant? In the first place, it gives you the conviction that all is well. Realizing that you have a monetary pad can assist you with exploring life's high points and low points all the more serenely and certainly. Second, it offers the force of decision. At the point when you're not secured by monetary limitations, you can make choices based on what makes you most joyful and generally satisfied, as opposed to what takes care of the bills. At long last, achieving independence from the rat race is innately engaging. It's a demonstration of your persistent effort, discipline, and savvy monetary preparation.

Understanding the significance of independence from the rat race is the initial step in charting a course for accomplishing it. It persuades us to make a move, make informed choices, and focus on our monetary prosperity. As we set out on this excursion together through "The Abundance Diagram," remember that independence from the rat race is achievable. With the right procedures and mentality, you can fabricate a life that is financially secure as well as wealthy in encounters and individual satisfaction.

Grasping Your Ongoing Monetary Circumstance

Prior to setting out on any excursion, realizing your beginning stage is urgent. The way to independence from the rat race is the same. An intensive comprehension of your ongoing monetary circumstances is the foundation upon which you can create your future financial wellbeing. This implies investigating your pay, costs, obligations, and reserve funds. It's tied in with being fiercely legitimate with yourself about where you stand monetarily, without judgment or self-analysis.

Begin by gathering together the entirety of your fiscal reports—ledgers, speculation accounts, financial records, credit archives, and some other records of your resources and liabilities. This exercise isn't just about numbers; it's tied in with making way for informed direction. By understanding your monetary inflows and outpourings, you can distinguish regions for development, like lessening superfluous costs or expanding your pay.

It is especially vital to dissect your obligations. Recognize exorbitant interest obligations, which can quickly disintegrate your riches, and reasonable obligations, which might be essential for a vital monetary arrangement. Realizing the thing that matters is significant for focusing on reimbursements and arriving at shrewd conclusions about utilizing obligations later on.

Similarly significant is figuring out your reserve funds and ventures. What amount do you have set aside for crises? Is it true or not that you are using money management for your drawn-out objectives, like retirement? This outline gives an unmistakable image of your monetary wellbeing and flexibility.

This step, while perhaps overwhelming, is enabling. It furnishes you with a reasonable, unvarnished gander at your funds, making way for the procedures and plans you will create all through this book. Understanding your ongoing monetary circumstances is the most important move toward rolling out significant improvements that line up with your objectives for independence from the rat race. As we push ahead, remember that this depiction of your funds is only a beginning stage. With the devices and information you'll acquire from "The Abundance Outline," you'll be able to advance your monetary circumstances and fabricate a protected, prosperous future.

The Brain Science of Riches

Accomplishing independence from the rat race isn't exclusively about dominating numbers or grasping business sectors; it's additionally well established in the brain research of riches. Your convictions, perspectives, and feelings about cash assume a pivotal role in the way you settle on monetary choices and, at last, in your capacity to accomplish independence from the rat race. This piece of our process is tied in with investigating the psychological boundaries that might be keeping you down and cultivating a mentality that upholds establishing long-term financial stability.

The brain science of abundance includes our thought process about, feel towards, and act with cash. Large numbers of these mentalities are formed right off the bat throughout everyday life, acquired from our families, and affected by our way of life and encounters. These firmly established convictions can prompt examples of conduct that either move us toward independence from the rat race or keep us caught in monetary frailty.

For example, a few people might convey a world view limited by fear, accepting there will never be sufficient cash, which prompts storing or outrageous thriftiness, keeping them from putting resources into valuable open doors that could develop their riches. Others could have a mentality of overflow, but need discipline, prompting overspending and undersaving. Perceiving these examples is the most vital move toward evolving them.

Changing your relationship with cash likewise includes developing a development mentality. This implies seeing monetary difficulties not as unfavorable impediments but rather as open doors for learning and development. It includes understanding that mishaps are essential for the excursion and that strength and flexibility are critical to beating them.

Besides, setting and keeping a positive monetary vision can propel and direct you toward your objectives. Representation procedures, certifications, and setting clear, reachable objectives can all assist with building up a positive monetary personality.

In this part, we dive into systems for conquering restricting convictions and personal conduct standards that block monetary achievement. We investigate how to supplant them with enabling convictions and propensities that help your journey to independence from the rat race. By getting it and changing your brain science around cash, you're not simply changing your monetary circumstance; you're changing your life. This investigation is an imperative part of "The Abundance Plan," offering bits of knowledge and devices for adjusting your outlook to your monetary objectives and laying the basis for enduring riches and opportunity.

Outline of the Abundance Diagram

As we stand at the limit of our excursion towards independence from the rat race, it's critical to have a guide—aa plan that guides us through the intricacies of individual budgets with clarity and reason. "The Abundance Diagram: Techniques for Independence from the Rat Race" is intended to be only that: a far-reaching guide that strolls you through each step of building, developing, and protecting your riches. This outline fills in as a review of the organized methodology we'll take to change your monetary life.

The Abundance Outline is organized around key standards and procedures that have been demonstrated to encourage monetary achievement. It's not just about effective money management or saving determinedly; it's about making a comprehensive monetary arrangement that incorporates all parts of your monetary life. From setting a strong monetary establishment by overseeing obligations and building a backup stash to cutting-edge, growing long-term financial stability systems including speculations, land, and business ventures, the plan covers the full range of an individual budget.

Every part of this book is devoted to a particular mainstay of independence from the rat race. We'll begin with the rudiments of planning and saving, continue on toward pay age and expansion, dive into venture procedures, investigate abundance conservation and expense arranging, and lastly, underscore the significance of attitude and constant improvement. Inside every section, central issues will feature noteworthy procedures, functional counsel, and bits of knowledge drawn from the present reality encounters of the individuals who have achieved independence from the rat race.

This outline plans to make way for what you can expect as you explore through the abundance diagram. It's intended to be both educational and persuasive, giving you the specialized information you want as well as the inspiration to apply that information in your own life. By understanding the general construction and objectives of the Outline, you'll be more ready to draw in with every section, execute its examples, and pursue informed choices that steer you towards monetary autonomy.

As we set out on this excursion together, remember that independence from the rat race isn't an objective yet a cycle. It requires responsibility, discipline, and an eagerness to learn and adjust. The Abundance Plan is your friend on this excursion, offering direction, support, and the devices you want to accomplish independence from the rat race. Allow this outline to be your challenge to investigate what lies ahead, with the commitment that the excursion we're going to embrace can change what is going on, however your life.

I

Chapter 1: Building a Solid Financial Foundation

The Basics of a Rainy Day Account
A backup stash is a monetary security net intended to cover unforeseen costs or monetary crises. The essence of having such an asset isn't in the event that crises occur, but when. Whether it's an unexpected employment cutback, a health-related crisis, or a startling home fix, life has an approach to introducing difficulties that can undermine your monetary security. A backup stash remains as a defense against these unanticipated occasions, guaranteeing that you can explore life's tempests without crashing your drawn-out monetary plans.

Deciding the Right Size for Your Backup Stash
The size of your rainy day account ought to mirror your ongoing way of life, monetary commitments, and the strength of your pay. A typical rule is to save to the point of covering three to a half years

7

of everyday costs. Nonetheless, in the event that your work circumstance is less steady or you have a family to help, holding back nothing cradle, like six to a year of costs, may be more judicious.

Systems for Building and Keeping Up with Your Assets
Building a secret stash requires discipline and an essential strategy. Begin by defining a month-to-month reserve fund objective, and treat this objective as a non-debatable cost in your financial plan. Computerizing your investment funds can eliminate the compulsion to skirt a month or spend the cash somewhere else. Indeed, even small commitments can accumulate over the long run, so begin with what you can manage and build your investment funds as your monetary circumstances change.

Where to Keep Your Rainy Day Account for Simple Access and Development
Openness is key for a rainy-day account. You should have the option to get to these assets rapidly and without punishment. High-return investment accounts are a well-known decision, as they offer preferable loan fees over conventional bank accounts while still giving simple access to your cash. Currency market records and momentary CDs can likewise be great choices, provided they don't lock your cash away for longer than you're okay with.

Taking Care of Crises Without Draining Your Asset
When confronted with a crisis, assess what is happening cautiously to decide whether it genuinely warrants dunking into your rainy day account. For less critical necessities, consider other subsidizing choices that won't think twice about the monetary security net. In the event that you should utilize your backup stash, focus on recharging it quickly. Change your financial plan, if essential, to divert

assets back into your crisis reserve funds until they're completely reestablished.

A backup stash isn't simply a monetary device; it's genuine serenity. It permits you to confront the startling with certainty, realizing that you're ready to deal with life's difficulties without forfeiting your monetary prosperity. Fabricating and keeping a backup stash is a crucial stage in making a strong monetary establishment, one that upholds both your ongoing necessities and your future objectives.

Making a Spending Plan That Works

A spending plan is something other than a rundown of your pay and costs; it is an instrument that engages you to assume command over your monetary fate. Making a spending plan that works is the main basic move toward building a strong monetary establishment. It includes understanding where your cash is going, settling on informed conclusions about your spending, and getting yourself in a position for a future where monetary pressure is limited and monetary objectives are reachable.

Definition and Significance of Planning

Planning is the most common way of making an arrangement for how you will spend and set aside your cash. It requires a reasonable comprehension of how much cash you procure versus the amount you spend. The significance of planning couldn't possibly be more significant; it is the foundation of individual monetary administration. A very well-created spending plan forestalls overspending, guarantees that investment fund objectives are met, and lays the foundation for financial wellbeing.

Moves toward making a spending plan

The most vital phase in making a financial plan is to follow your pay and costs over a set period, normally a month. This following ought to incorporate all kinds of revenue and all costs, regardless of how little. When you have an unmistakable image of your monetary situation, classify your costs into fixed (e.g., lease, home loan, utilities) and variable (e.g., feasting out, diversion) classifications. This qualification distinguishes regions where changes can be made.

Then, put forth monetary objectives, both present-day and long-term. These objectives will direct your planning choices and assist with focusing on your spending and saving. Considering your objectives, dispense your pay towards your costs, reserve funds, and obligation reimbursement, guaranteeing that your spending doesn't surpass your pay.

Altering your financial plan to accommodate your way of life
A spending plan ought to mirror your own qualities, way of life, and monetary objectives. There's actually no need to focus on limiting yourself, but rather on making purposeful decisions with your cash. Alter your financial plan by disbursing assets to what makes the biggest difference to you, whether that is travel, leisure activities, or putting resources into your future. Keep in mind that a spending plan that works for another person may not work for you; the key is tracking down an equilibrium that accommodates what is happening.

Instruments and Applications for Powerful Planning
There are various instruments and applications accessible to assist with planning, from straightforward calculation sheets to refined monetary arrangement programming. These devices can automate a significant part of the following and classifying process, making it more straightforward to keep track of your funds. They can likewise give important insights into your spending examples and assist you with changing your spending plan as your monetary circumstances develop.

Normal Planning Difficulties and How to Defeat Them
Planning difficulties are normal, from unforeseen costs to fluctuating pay. Conquering these difficulties requires adaptability and

flexibility. Permit your financial plan to be adaptable, changing on a case-by-case basis to accommodate life's capriciousness. Assemble a just-in-case account to manage unforeseen costs without crashing your financial plan. Above all, remain focused on your monetary objectives, and don't allow transitory difficulties to put you down.

Making a spending plan that works is the most important move toward achieving monetary steadiness and opportunity. A powerful cycle develops between your life and your objectives. By carving out the opportunity to figure out your funds, put forth clear objectives, and make informed choices about your cash, you're laying the groundwork for a safe monetary future.

Obligation The Executive Techniques
In the mission for independence from the rat race, overseeing and, in the end, wiping out obligations is an urgent part. Obligations, particularly exorbitant interest obligations, can fundamentally thwart your capacity to create financial momentum and accomplish monetary objectives. In any case, with the right systems, overseeing and taking care of obligations can turn into an enabling piece of your monetary excursion, not a burden.

Figuring out Various Sorts of Obligation
Not all obligations are equivalent. There are different kinds of obligations, each with its own arrangement of terms, loan costs, and suggestions for your monetary wellbeing. Gotten obligations are attached to a resource, like a home loan for a home or a credit for a vehicle, and regularly have lower financing costs. Debts without collateral, similar to charge card obligations and individual credits, are not supported by resources and frequently accompany higher financing costs. Understanding the distinctions between these kinds of obligations is vital for focusing on which obligations to take care of first.

Focusing on Obligation Reimbursement

The way to a viable obligation for the executives is to focus on your obligations so that they set aside the most cash and open up income as fast as could be expected. Procedures like the obligation snowball strategy, where you take care of obligations from littlest to biggest, can give you energy and pride. On the other hand, the obligation torrential slide technique centers around taking care of obligations with the most noteworthy financing costs first, possibly setting aside more cash over the long haul. The right system for you will depend on your own inclinations and monetary circumstances.

Haggling with Banks and Combining Obligations
Here and there, overseeing obligations requires haggling with loan bosses to bring down financing costs or change reimbursement terms. Numerous lenders will work with purchasers to guarantee obligations are reimbursed. Obligation union, through an individual credit or equilibrium move Mastercard, can likewise be a suitable procedure. It includes consolidating different obligations into one, in a perfect world, at a lower loan fee, making installments more sensible, and getting a good deal on interest.

Making a Practical Arrangement to Take Care of Obligations
A fruitful obligation reimbursement plan is sensible and maintainable. It begins with surveying your financial plan to decide the amount you can stand to put towards obligations every month without forfeiting fundamental costs. From that point, set clear, reachable focuses for obligation decrease, and keep tabs on your development. Celebrating little triumphs enroute can assist with keeping up with inspiration.

Remaining inspired and keeping tabs on your development
Obligation reimbursement is often a drawn-out try, and remaining roused can challenge. Watching out for the award—independence from the rat race—is fundamental. Picturing your advancement, whether through outlines, applications, or normal surveys of your budget summaries, can build up the positive effect of your endeavors.

Furthermore, consider finding an emotionally supportive network, for example, a monetary responsibility accomplice or a local area of individuals with comparable objectives, to empower you enroute.

Powerful obligation The board isn't just about taking care of what you owe; it's tied in with changing your relationship with cash and settling on essential choices that line up with your independence from the rat race objectives. By grasping your obligations, focusing on reimbursement, haggling better terms, and remaining propelled, you're not simply clearing obligations; you're fabricating an establishment for a safer and prosperous monetary future.

Protection: Safeguarding Your Resources
In the texture of independence from the rat race, protection fills in as a basic wellbeing net, intended to shield you and your resources from unexpected occasions that can have wrecking monetary effects. It's a fundamental part of a strong monetary establishment, offering true serenity and security in a world loaded with vulnerabilities. Understanding the basic types of insurance for monetary security, deciding the right inclusion for your requirements, and exploring the intricacies of contract terms are urgent moves toward shielding your excursion toward monetary freedom.

Kinds of Protection Basics for Monetary Assurance
There are a few kinds of protection that are fundamental for complete monetary insurance. Health care coverage covers clinical costs, a need given the significant expense of medical services. Extra security accommodates your friends and family in case of your troublesome passing, while handicap protection replaces a piece of your pay. Would it be a good idea for you to become unfit to work? Property protection, including mortgage holders or leaseholders protection, shields your home and assets from harm or burglary. Collision protection is expected for drivers and safeguards against the monetary results of car crashes. Each kind of protection assumes a special role in a balanced monetary security plan.

Deciding the Right Inclusion for Your Necessities

Picking the right protection Inclusion is a difficult exercise between being over-safeguarded and under-guaranteed. It requires a cautious evaluation of your own circumstances, resources, and chance elements. For instance, how much disaster protection you want depends on elements like your pay, obligations, and the monetary necessities of wards. Essentially, the perfect proportion of property protection ought to take care of the substitution expense of your home and assets. Routinely reconsidering your protection needs guarantees that your inclusion advances with your life conditions.

Understanding strategy terms and staying away from normal errors

Insurance contracts can be intricate, and it's critical to comprehend the agreements to keep away from normal entanglements. This includes knowing your deductibles, the occasions covered and prohibited, and how to document a case. Mistaken assumptions about inclusion can prompt expensive astonishments when you least anticipate them. Teaching yourself the particulars of your arrangements, clarifying pressing issues, and perusing the fine print are pivotal steps toward making informed protection choices.

Looking for Protection and Contrasting Suppliers

Not all protection suppliers are equivalent, and looking can prompt huge reserve funds and better inclusion. Analyze statements from different suppliers, taking into account the cost as well as the inclusion offered, client care notoriety, and case process. Free surveys and evaluations can give important insights into a supplier's unwavering quality and execution.

Routinely Investigating and Refreshing Your Inclusion

Life is dynamic, and your protection and inclusion ought to mirror those changes. Routinely assessing and refreshing your protection guarantees that your inclusion stays in line with your on-going necessities. Critical life-altering situations like marriage, the introduction of a youngster, buying a home, or beginning a business are triggers for a strategy survey. This proactive methodology guarantees that your protection inclusion keeps on offering the security you really want as you draw nearer to achieving independence from the rat race.

Protection isn't simply an expense; it's an interest in your monetary prosperity and true serenity. By cautiously choosing the right sorts and measures of insurance, figuring out your contracts, and routinely looking into your inclusion, you're finding significant ways to shield yourself and your resources from the flighty, guaranteeing that your way to independence from the rat race stays secure.

2

Chapter 2: Income Generation and Diversification

Investigating Different Surges of Pay

In the present monetary scene, depending exclusively on a solitary pay source is, as of now, not an assurance of monetary soundness, not to mention independence from the rat race. The idea of producing different surges of pay is pivotal for creating financial wellbeing, diminishing monetary risk, and accomplishing a safer monetary future. This segment digs into the significance of expanding your pay and gives noteworthy methodologies for recognizing and fostering extra pay sources.

Understanding the Worth of Various Revenue Sources

The essential advantage of having different revenue streams is monetary strength. In a dubious work market, extra pay sources can provide a security net that protects you against employment cutbacks, financial slumps, or unforeseen costs. Past security, different revenue streams can speed up your way to independence from the rat race, empowering you to contribute more, save more, and accomplish your monetary objectives sooner.

Distinguishing open doors for extra pay

The journey to enhancing your pay starts with distinguishing valuable open doors that line up with your abilities, interests, and accessible time. This could mean outsourcing in your expert field, chasing after a side interest that can be adapted, or putting resources into pay-producing resources. The key is to begin with what you know and are energetic about, as this improves the probability of accomplishment and supportability.

Adjusting Time Between Essential Work and Side Jobs

While seeking out various revenue sources, it's fundamental to maintain equilibrium to forestall burnout. This includes using time productively, defining clear limits, and focusing on undertakings. Keep in mind that the objective is to upgrade your monetary prosperity, not to think twice about wellbeing or personal satisfaction. Finding the right equilibrium might require experimentation; however, it is feasible with ingenuity and discipline.

Genuine Instances of Effective Pay Broadening

Drawing motivation from genuine models can give important insights into the cycle and advantages of pay expansion. Whether an educator begins a mentoring business, an IT proficient who fosters a product application, or a craftsman who sells their work on the web, these accounts feature the range of ways people can make extra revenue sources.

Procedures for Scaling and Mechanizing Revenue Sources

As your extra revenue streams start to develop, investigating ways of scaling and computerizing them can prompt more prominent monetary benefits with less exertion over the long run. This could include re-appropriating specific assignments, utilizing innovation, or putting resources into assets that upgrade efficiency. The goal is to assemble proficient frameworks that permit your revenue streams to thrive, in any event, when you're not effectively chipping away at them.

Investigating different surges of pay is something other than a system for monetary security; it's an excursion towards monetary freedom and strengthening. By utilizing your abilities, embracing business ventures, and pursuing key decisions, you can fabricate a differentiated pay portfolio that upholds your monetary objectives and way of life yearnings.

Putting resources into your vote and instruction

In a quickly developing position market, putting resources into your vocation and training isn't simply a pathway to self-awareness; it's an essential move towards monetary freedom. This venture is tied in with upgrading your worth in the commercial center, getting higher pay potential, and guaranteeing long-term employability. We should investigate the significance of nonstop learning, expertise improvement, and how to turn your expert development into monetary achievement.

The Significance of Ceaseless Acquisition and Expertise Improvement

The groundwork for professional success and monetary development lies in a guarantee of nonstop learning. In the present unique monetary climate, new advancements, approaches, and industry guidelines arise at a remarkable speed. Remaining refreshed with these progressions and growing your range of abilities can separate you in the gig market, opening doors to new opportunities and higher procuring potential.

Distinguishing Appeal Abilities and Ventures

To augment the profit from your instructive venture, center around gaining abilities and information that are popular. This requires examination and prescience; search for patterns in work market information, proficient distributions, and industry news. Fields like innovation, medical care, and environmentally friendly power, for instance, have shown reliable development and interest for gifted experts. By adjusting your instructive interests to these areas, you can situate yourself for progress in areas ready for future development.

Utilizing Proficient Organizations and Mentorships

Fabricating and supporting an expert organization is a strong procedure in your vocation improvement ammunition stockpile. Systems administration can give insider information about employment opportunities, industry patterns, and valuable open doors for joint effort. Furthermore, looking for mentorships can offer customized direction, vocation counsel, and the insight of involvement. These connections can be instrumental in exploring your vocation and revealing open doors for progression and pay development.

Haggling for more significant compensation and better advantages

One of the most immediate methods for making an interpretation of your profession's interest in monetary profit is through viable discussion. Equipped with upgraded abilities and capabilities, you're in a more grounded position to arrange more significant compensation, better advantages, and ideal business terms. Readiness is critical; arm yourself with information on industry compensation norms, articulate your incentive clearly, and be prepared to talk about your accomplishments and the extra advantages you offer that might be of some value.

Offsetting professional success with individual prosperity

While chasing after professional success, it's pivotal to keep an eye on your own prosperity. Burnout can sabotage both your expert achievement and monetary objectives. Practice taking care of oneself, put down stopping points, and guarantee that your drive for vocation development doesn't come to the detriment of your wellbeing or individual life. Keep in mind that genuine independence from the rat race likewise implies having the opportunity and wellbeing to partake in the rewards of so much hard work.

Putting resources into your profession and instruction is a continuous interaction that requires foreknowledge, devotion, and an essential methodology. By zeroing in on popularity abilities, utilizing your organization, haggling really, and keeping a good overall arrangement, you can change your profession direction and prepare for independence from the rat race and achievement.

Beginning a side business

Leaving on the excursion of beginning a side business makes you ready for extra pay as well as paves the way for individual satisfaction and the potential for monetary freedom. This adventure requires a mix of enthusiasm, versatility, and key preparation. We should explore the essential moves toward transforming your innovative dreams into the real world, guaranteeing that your side business contributes emphatically to your monetary outline.

Evaluating Your Abilities and Interests for Business Thoughts

The beginning of a fruitful side business lies in the convergence of your abilities, interests, and market interests. Start by considering what you're great at, what you appreciate doing, and how these can take care of an issue or satisfy a need on the lookout. Whether it's creating carefully assembled merchandise, offering proficient consultancy, or utilizing your educated website composition, the best business thoughts frequently originate from your current abilities and interests.

Approving Your Business Thoughts and Market Interest

Prior to plunging deeply into your business, it's pivotal to approve your thoughts against market interest. Research your interest group, grasp their requirements, and survey how well your item or administration addresses those issues. Apparatuses like web-based overviews, market examinations, and criticism from potential clients can provide priceless experiences. This step guarantees that your endeavor has a battling opportunity in the cutthroat scene, limiting dangers and adjusting your endeavors to genuine market open doors.

Rudiments of Business Arranging and Startup Funds

A strong, field-tested strategy is your guide to progress, illustrating your business objectives, procedures, and how you intend to accomplish them. This plan ought to incorporate a definite investigation of your objective market, a reasonable incentive, promotion and deal methodologies, and, critically, a monetary arrangement. Understanding startup costs, progressing costs, income projections, and earning back the original investment are crucial to dealing with your side business' funds successfully. It's tied in with finding some kind of harmony between desire and authenticity, guaranteeing your business can develop without risking your monetary strength.

Showcasing Your Business on a Tight Spending Plan

In the underlying stages, your showcasing spending plan might be restricted; however, that doesn't mean you can't shake things up. Computerized advertising offers financially savvy channels to contact your crowd, from online entertainment stages and email promotion to content showcasing and website design enhancement systems. The key is to make drawing-in, esteem-driven content that reverberates with your interest group, fabricating a brand presence that draws in clients naturally. Organizing, both on the web and disconnected, can likewise open new doors without burning through every last dollar.

Difficulties of Business Ventures and How to Conquer Them

Beginning and maintaining a side business is full of difficulties, from using time productively and monetary tensions to the vulnerability of the business. The way to beat these obstacles is versatility, a strong organization, and a readiness to adjust. Try not to avoid looking for exhortations from coaches, individual business people, or even clients. Embrace disappointment as a learning opportunity, and utilize these bits of knowledge to refine your plan of action. Keep in mind that each mishap is a step in the right direction in camouflage, showing you important illustrations that make you ready for future achievement.

Beginning a side business is a strong step towards differentiating your pay and achieving independence from the rat race. It consolidates your own assets and interests with the discipline of key preparation and monetary administration. By moving toward this endeavor with an unmistakable arrangement, a sharp comprehension of the market, and a versatile outlook, you can fabricate a side business that creates extra pay as well as brings gigantic individual fulfillment and development.

Recurring, automated revenue Thoughts
Chasing independence from the rat race, making wellsprings of recurring, automated revenue is likened to sowing seeds that develop into organic product-bearing trees. These revenue streams require a forthright venture of time, cash, or both, yet once settled, they can possibly furnish a consistent progression of pay with insignificant continuous exertion. This segment investigates the idea of automated revenue, divulges an assortment of automated revenue thoughts, and guides you on overseeing and developing these sources.

Characterizing Recurring, Automated Revenue, and Its Advantages
Automated revenue is procured from adventures in which an individual doesn't effectively elaborate on an everyday premise. The charm of recurring, automated revenue lies in its capacity to produce profit after some time, liberating you from the imperatives of conventional regular work and giving monetary security and freedom. This type of pay can supplement your dynamic pay, speeding

up your way to accomplishing your monetary objectives and permitting you more opportunity to pursue your interests.

Instances of Recurring Sources of Income

There are various ways to produce recurring, automated revenue, each with its own arrangement of benefits and contemplations. Venture pay from stocks, securities, or profit-paying resources offers a method for bringing in your cash to work for you. Land speculations, whether through investment properties or land venture trusts (REITs), provide an unmistakable resource that can be seen in value while creating rental income. Computerized items, for example, digital books, online courses, or programming, can be made once and sold over and over again to new clients. Partner promoting and publicizing income from a blog or YouTube channel are likewise famous techniques for procuring automated revenue, utilizing content creation to fabricate an income stream over the long run.

Beginning Speculation and Exertion Required

While recurring sources of income might require negligible work to keep up with, they frequently require a critical forthright venture of time, cash, or both. For instance, buying an investment property requires capital, while making a computerized item requires time and skill. The way to progress is by choosing an automated revenue plan that lines up with your inclinations, abilities, and monetary circumstances. It's additionally vital to conduct an exhaustive examination and potentially look for counsel from specialists in the field to limit gambles and expand returns.

Overseeing and developing automated revenue sources

Compelling administration of your automated revenue sources is critical to guaranteeing their life span and benefit. This could include customary observing of speculation portfolios, keeping up with and overhauling investment properties, or refreshing advanced items to keep them applicable. Also, reinvesting benefits from your recurring sources of income can intensify their development, further supporting your profit. Broadening your recurring, automated revenue sources is likewise prudent to spread chance and increase your monetary strength.

Charge Ramifications of Recurring, Automated Revenue

It's essential to know about the expense suggestions related to recurring, automated revenue, as they can change contingent upon the kind of pay and your area. At times, automated revenue can be charged at an unexpected rate in comparison to dynamic pay. Talking with a duty expert can give you clarity on the most proficient method to deal with these commitments productively and exploit any tax reductions or derivations accessible to you.

Automated revenue offers a way to independence from the rat race by giving monetary benefits without a relative expansion in continuous work. By cautiously choosing, making due, and developing your recurring sources of income, you can construct a strong monetary establishment that upholds your way of life and long-term objectives. Whether through ventures, land, computerized items, or different roads, the way to progress in recurring, automated revenue is to begin with a well-defined course of action, remain committed, and persistently look for open doors for development and enhancement.

Land Money Management Fundamentals

Land putting remains a foundation in the structure of growing long-term financial stability, offering a substantial way to create automated revenue and achieve independence from the rat race. This endeavor, notwithstanding, requires a sharp comprehension of the market, an essential way to deal with speculation, and a consciousness of the monetary ramifications. In this part, we'll explore the basics of land financial planning, helping you lay the basis for a productive and practical land portfolio.

Various kinds of land ventures

The domain of land offers an assortment of speculation-opening doors, each with its own possible rewards and dangers. Private land includes properties like houses, condos, and excursion rentals, offering the chance of rental pay or benefits from resale. Business land, including office spaces, retail stores, and stockrooms, can turn out to have higher revenue potential and longer rent terms. Land speculation trusts (REITs) permit financial backers to enter the housing market through the acquisition of offers in land portfolios, offering liquidity and expansion without the requirement for direct property from the board.

Dissecting Land: Potential Open Doors

Fruitful land and effective money management depend on your capacity to examine properties and economic situations. Key elements to consider include area, property condition, market patterns, and likely rental pay or resale esteem. Monetary measurements, for example, income, profit from venture (return on initial capital investment), and rate of return are basic in evaluating the feasibility and productivity of a speculation. Directing an exhaustive and reasonable level of effort, including property examinations and lawful checks, can assist with moderating dangers and illuminate your speculation choices.

Supporting Choices for Land Speculation

Getting support is an essential move toward a land venture. Customary home loans, confidential advances, and land crowdfunding are among the funding choices accessible to financial backers. Every choice accompanies its own arrangement of terms, loan fees, and capability prerequisites. Understanding the expense of funding, including initial installments, financing costs, and credit terms, is fundamental to deciding the general productivity of your venture.

Overseeing Properties and Managing Inhabitants

Powerful property for the executives is vital to augmenting the profit from your land speculations. This includes finding and checking inhabitants, setting and gathering rent, keeping up with the property, and taking care of any legitimate or monetary issues that emerge. For people who don't really want to oversee properties straightforwardly, recruiting a property executive organization can be a practical alternative, yet with related costs.

Long-haul methodologies for land portfolio development
Building a productive land portfolio is a drawn-out endeavor that requires vital preparation and continuous administration. Enhancing your ventures across various kinds of properties and markets can assist with relieving risk and boosting returns. Reinvesting benefits, utilizing value, and remaining informed about market patterns and potential open doors are urgent systems for portfolio development and outcome in land money management.

Land-effective money management offers a strong road for creating financial stability and producing automated revenue; however, it requires cautious preparation, informed navigation, and tenacious administration. By figuring out the fundamentals of land venture, from investigating open doors and tying down supporting to overseeing properties and planning for development, you can leave on a path that prompts independence from the rat race and the acknowledgment of your growing strong financial foundation objectives.

3

Chapter 3: Investment Strategies for Wealth Building

Grasping the Securities Exchange

The securities exchange, frequently seen as the heartbeat of the monetary world, is a mind-boggling biological system where portions of freely held organizations are given, purchased, and sold. It tends to be an integral asset for establishing long-term financial stability, offering the potential for huge profits from speculation. This segment demystifies the securities exchange, directing you through its essentials and systems for effective financial planning.

Nuts and bolts of the Securities Exchange Effective financial planning

Putting resources into the financial exchange starts with understanding what stocks are: portions of proprietorship in an organization. At the point when you purchase a stock, you're purchasing a piece of that organization, including the option to partake in its benefits and a say in its corporate choices, regularly through deciding on significant issues. The financial exchange is comprised of trades, similar to the New York Stock Exchange (NYSE) and the Nasdaq, where stocks are traded. The cost of each stock varies in view of market interest and is affected by the organization's exhibition, monetary factors, and market sentiment.

Investigating stocks for speculation

Picking the right stocks requires investigation and examination. Key examinations include assessing an organization's monetary well-being, market position, and development potential by inspecting budget summaries, income, profit, future development, return on value, and other information. Specialized examination, then again, centers around designs in stock value developments and exchanging volumes to foresee future action. A fruitful financial backer frequently joins the two ways to settle on informed choices.

Broadening Inside the Securities Exchange

One of the critical systems for moderating gambles in financial exchange money management is expansion—spreading your ventures across different areas, enterprises, and geographic areas. This approach shields your portfolio from instability, as the under-performance of one speculation can be counterbalanced by the outcome of another. Putting resources into a blend of little-cap, mid-cap, and huge-cap stocks, as well as thinking about worldwide stocks, can additionally broaden your portfolio.

Long-haul versus momentary specification procedures

Securities exchange financial backers, for the most part, fall into two classifications: long-haul and momentary financial backers. Long-haul financial backers, frequently called "purchase and hold" financial backers, buy stocks fully intent on holding them for quite a long time or even many years, profiting from building interest and development over the long haul. Momentary financial backers, or brokers, trade stocks rapidly to benefit from market changes. While transient exchanging can offer speedy returns, it's less secure and calls for greater investment and aptitude.

Dangers and Compensations of Securities Exchange Money Management

Putting resources into the securities exchange offers the potential for exceptional yields, altogether outperforming expansion after some time, which is fundamental for creating financial wellbeing. In any case, it likewise accompanies chances. Market unpredictability can prompt abrupt and huge misfortunes, and individual organizations can fizzle, affecting their stock worth. A restrained methodology, a well-informed speculation procedure, and a broadened portfolio are critical to dealing with these dangers and making progress in the financial exchange.

Understanding the securities exchange is the most vital move towards utilizing it for establishing a strong financial foundation. With information, persistence, and an essential methodology, financial backers can explore the intricacies of the market, settling on informed choices that lead to monetary development and strength.

Securities, shared assets, and ETFs

Enhancing your speculation portfolio is significant for limiting risk while augmenting likely returns, and securities, shared assets, and trade-exchanged reserves (ETFs) assume vital roles in accomplishing this equilibrium. This part investigates the qualities, advantages, and contemplations of putting resources into these instruments, giving an exhaustive comprehension that will engage your speculation choices.

Prologue to Bonds and Their Part in Establishing a Strong Financial Foundation

Securities are fixed-pay speculations where a financial backer credits cash to an element (corporate or legislative) that gets the assets for a characterized period at a variable or fixed loan cost.

Securities act as a more steady partner to the instability of the financial exchange, offering ordinary pay through interest installments and the arrival of head-to-head development. They are fundamental for financial backers looking to protect capital and create consistent pay, making them a key part of a differentiated speculation portfolio.

Advantages of Putting Resources into Shared Assets

Shared reserves pool cash from numerous financial backers to buy a differentiated arrangement of stocks, securities, or different protections, oversaw by proficient asset chiefs. This broadening and expert administration offer a few benefits, including admittance to a more extensive scope of speculations than most people could bear or oversee all alone, decreased risk through expansion, and the comfort of having specialists settle on venture choices. Shared reserves are reasonable for financial backers who favor a hands-off approach or are hoping to differentiate with negligible exertion.

The Benefits of Trade-Exchanged Assets (ETFs)

ETFs are speculation finances exchanged on stock trades, similar to stocks, and hold resources like stocks, products, or bonds. They consolidate the expanded arrangement of a common asset effortlessly by exchanging it with stocks, offering adaptability, lower cost proportions, and duty productivity. ETFs are especially engaging for their capacity to be traded all through the exchanging day at market cost, giving financial backers command over their speculation timing and systems.

Expanding with Securities, Common Assets, and ETFs

Consolidating securities, common assets, and ETFs into your portfolio can essentially lessen risk by spreading ventures across different resource classes, areas, and geological areas. This enhancement system mitigates the effect of terrible showings in any single speculation. For example, while stocks might offer higher development potential, securities can provide soundness and pay, with common assets and ETFs considering expansive openness to a range of ventures.

Evaluating Chance and Return in These Ventures

While securities, shared assets, and ETFs are for the most part viewed as safer than individual stocks, they are not without risks. Securities face credit hazard and loan cost risk, while common assets and ETFs are liable to showcase chance and the executives risk. It's significant to evaluate the gamble return profile of these speculations, taking into account factors like your venture skyline, risk resistance, and monetary objectives. Understanding these components will guide you in choosing the right blend of securities, common assets, and ETFs to adjust your portfolio and accomplish your financial stability targets.

Putting resources into securities, shared assets, and ETFs offers a pathway to enhancing your venture portfolio, offsetting risk with likely returns. By understanding the novel qualities and advantages of every, you can settle on informed choices that line up with your monetary objectives, risk resilience, and speculation technique, making you ready for a safer and prosperous monetary future.

Land Speculation Methodologies

Land speculation remains a reliable road for abundance creation, offering various pathways to produce pay and capital appreciation. With its remarkable mix of unmistakable resources, potential for influence, and pay expansion, land presents a convincing open door for financial backers hoping to widen their portfolio past conventional stocks and bonds. This segment dives into the central methodologies of land ventures, directing you through the subtleties of creating financial momentum through property.

Outline of Land as a Speculation Methodology

Putting resources into land includes buying property to produce rental income, accomplish capital development, or both. Not at all like stocks and bonds, land is an unmistakable resource, offering the double benefit of being a fence against expansion and a method for portfolio broadening. Land ventures can range from private properties, business land, and land advancement to land speculation trusts (REITs), each with an unmistakable gamble to bring profiles back.

Direct Possession versus Land Speculation Gatherings

Direct possession alludes to buying property inside and out, offering unlimited authority over the resource, its pay, and its appreciation. This approach requires critical capital, skill in property for the executives, and a high capacity to bear the intricacies of property proprietorship. On the other hand, land venture gatherings (REIGs) permit financial backers to purchase partakes in an expertly overseen arrangement of properties, furnishing openness to land with less active contribution. This model suits financial backers looking for the pay and appreciation capability of land without the requests of direct administration.

REITs: A Method for Putting Resources into Land Without Claiming Property

Land Speculation Trusts (REITs) offer a more open section point into land ventures, permitting people to put resources into the arrangement of land resources through the acquisition of public offers. REITs consolidate the liquidity of corporate securities with the strength and pay capability of land, paying out a greater part of their available pay as profits to investors. This design makes REITs an alluring choice for those hoping to broaden into land with lower capital prerequisites and adaptability.

Utilizing Land Money Management

Influence, or the utilization of acquired cash flow to build the likely return of a speculation, is an integral asset in effective financial planning. By supporting a part of the property price tag with an obligation, financial backers can enhance their profit from speculation compared with purchasing the property by and large. Nonetheless, influence likewise increments risk, as the expense of acquiring can offset the pay and enthusiasm for the property under antagonistic circumstances.

Assessing land speculation Open doors

Effective land money management requires a tireless assessment of speculation, which opens amazing doors. Key contemplations incorporate area, market patterns, property condition, and monetary examination of pay potential versus costs. Understanding the neighborhood housing market, evaluating property estimation precisely, and computing income and profit from speculation are basic moves toward distinguishing properties that line up with your venture objectives and hazard resistance.

Land speculation procedures encompass a wide range of chances, each offering particular benefits and difficulties. Whether through direct proprietorship, REIGs, or utilizing, the way to progress in land putting lies in careful examination, key preparation, and a reasonable comprehension of your monetary goals. By cautiously choosing and overseeing land ventures, you can take advantage of this powerful resource class's capability to upgrade your long-term financial stability venture.

Cryptographic money and elective speculations

In the steadily developing scene of speculation, valuable open doors, digital currency, and elective ventures have arisen as unique parts of a differentiated portfolio. These resources, while conveying a higher gambling profile, offer special advantages, including the potential for significant returns and further enhancement beyond conventional business sectors. This segment investigates the complexities of putting resources into digital currency and other elective resources, giving experiences to successfully explore these mind-boggling waters.

Figuring out digital currency as a speculation

Digital money is computerized or virtual cash that involves cryptography for security and works freely for a national bank. As a venture, it has stood out for its fast appreciation and the progressive blockchain innovation that supports it. In any case, the digital money market is described by high unpredictability, administrative vulnerabilities, and advancing mechanical scenes. Financial backers intrigued by cryptographic money ought to go for a gold comprehension of blockchain innovation, market patterns, and the particular dangers and open doors each computerized currency presents.

Dangers and Expected Compensations of Putting Resources into Cryptographic Money

The unstable idea of digital forms of money can prompt huge vacillations in esteem, offering the chance of significant yields yet additionally presenting a significant gamble to financial backers. The market is impacted by variables like mechanical headways, administrative changes, market feeling, and hypothesis. While the potential for outsized returns exists, financial backers should be ready for the chance of huge misfortunes and direct industrious examination to make informed choices.

Investigating Elective Speculations (Craftsmanship, Collectibles, and so on.)

Past digital currency, the domain of elective ventures incorporates a wide exhibit of resources, including craftsmanship, collectibles, and valuable metals, and that's just the beginning. These ventures offer one-of-a kind advantages, like stylish worth, actual substance, and possible support against expansion. Nonetheless, they additionally require specific information to explore, as their worth can be affected by variables like unique cases, conditions, authentic importance, and market interest.

Broadening Your Portfolio with Elective Ventures

Integrating elective interests into your portfolio can upgrade expansion, lessen, generally speaking, risk, and possibly open new sources of profit. These resources frequently show a low relationship with customary monetary business sectors, meaning they can give strength during times of securities exchange unpredictability. Notwithstanding, financial backers ought to consider the liquidity, valuation difficulties, and longer speculation skylines frequently connected with elective resources.

Instructions to Assess an Elective Venture Open doors

Assessing elective ventures requires a mix of exploration, skill, and a reasonable level of effort. For craftsmanship and collectibles, this could include talking with specialists, confirming things, and understanding the verifiable and social factors that drive esteem. For valuable metals and collectibles, checking market patterns and request pointers is pivotal. No matter what the resource class, financial backers ought to evaluate the potential for appreciation, the dangers implied, and how the speculation fits inside their more extensive monetary procedure.

Digital currency and elective ventures address an outskirts in the speculation scene, offering valuable open doors for development and expansion. While exploring these business sectors requires alertness, an educated and key methodology can uncover significant open doors for financial backers able to investigate past conventional resource classes. By understanding the one-of-a kind qualities and dangers of these speculations, you can settle on choices that line up with your monetary objectives and hazard resistance, possibly improving your portfolio's exhibition and flexibility.

Risk The board and expansion

In the domain of financial planning, risk management and broadening are not only methodologies but rather fundamental teachings that defend your abundance and advance your portfolio's true capacity. These standards act as the bedrock of sound speculation reasoning, assisting financial backers with exploring the vulnerabilities of the market while chasing after their monetary objectives. This part enlightens you on the basic significance of these practices and offers noteworthy experiences for incorporating them into your venture approach.

The Significance of Hazards The board of effective financial planning

Risk on the board implies distinguishing, surveying, and focusing on taking a chance, followed by the planned utilization of assets to limit or control the probability and effect of lamentable occasions. With regards to effective money management, it implies understanding the dangers associated with every speculation, how they relate to your monetary objectives, and the means you can take to moderate them. Compelling gambles the executives safeguard against expected misfortunes as well as guarantee that your venture choices line up with your gamble resistance and monetary goals.

Procedures for Expanding Your Venture Portfolio

Expansion is the essential act of spreading speculations across different monetary instruments, businesses, and different classes to diminish openness to any single resource or chance. The objective of broadening isn't really to boost returns, but rather to restrict the effect of unpredictability on your portfolio. By putting resources into a blend of resource classes, like stocks, bonds, land, and digital forms of money, you can accomplish a more steady, generally speaking, exhibition, as the underperformance of certain ventures is probably going to be balanced by the more grounded execution of others.

Adjusting Chance and Award

Integral to the venture interaction is the harmony between hazards and prizes. For the most part, higher-risk ventures offer the potential for better yields, while lower-risk speculations will quite often yield more unassuming returns. Figuring out your own gamble resilience—your capacity and readiness to persevere through market unpredictability—is significant in deciding the right equilibrium for your portfolio. This understanding ought to direct your venture decisions, guaranteeing that you are OK with the degree of chance you are taking on in quest for your monetary objectives.

Utilizing Resource Portion to Oversee Speculation Chance

Resource designation is the method involved with splitting a speculation portfolio between various resource classifications, like stocks, bonds, land, and money. This methodology depends on the reason that different resource classes perform differently under different economic situations. Compelling resource allotment relies upon precisely surveying your gamble resilience, speculation skyline, and monetary objectives, then fitting the conveyance of resources in your portfolio to match your one-of-a kind profile. Consistently returning to and changing your resource distribution guarantees that your portfolio stays lined up with your drawn-out goals.

Ordinary Portfolio Audit and Change

The monetary market's dynamic nature expects financial backers to survey and change their portfolios occasionally. This interaction includes reevaluating your monetary objectives, risk resistance, and the presentation of your ventures. Changes in life conditions, monetary circumstances, or monetary objectives might require adjustments to your portfolio to guarantee it stays strategically situated to meet your goals. Standard surveys permit you to make remedial moves, for example, rebalancing your resource portion or diverting speculations to keep up with your essential vision.

Risk management and broadening are fundamental apparatuses in the financial backer's arms stockpile, empowering you to seek after abundance creation while alleviating the dangers innate in the monetary business sectors. By embracing these standards, you can explore the intricacies of money management with certainty, constructing a versatile and very well-considered portfolio that is prepared to face the hardships of instability and benefit from valuable open doors for development.

4

Chapter 4: Wealth Preservation and Tax Planning

Domain Arranging Fundamentals

Bequest arranging is an essential part of abundance safeguarding, guaranteeing that your resources are secured and passed on as indicated by your wants for your demise or crippling. A long way from being a worry just for the well-off, bequest arranging is a fundamental interaction for anybody trying to get their monetary inheritance and accommodate their friends and family. This segment dives into the fundamentals of bequest arranging, illustrating the vital components and methodologies to shield your resources and guarantee they benefit the ideal individuals with impeccable timing.

Understanding the Significance of Bequest Arranging

Bequest arranging includes something beyond conveying your resources in the afterlife. It's a far-reaching way to deal with dealing with your monetary wellbeing, defending your family's future, and limiting the lawful obstacles and expenses they might confront. Viable home arranging guarantees that your desires are respected, lessens the weight on your friends and family, and can essentially impact the monetary prosperity of people in the future.

Key parts of a home arrangement

A very organized home arrangement incorporates a few key parts: a will, trusts, legal authority, and medical services mandates. A will is the foundation, determining how your resources ought to be disbursed and who will deal with the domain. Confides in offering more command over how and when your resources are conveyed, giving advantages like duty proficiency and resource security. A general legal authority names somebody to deal with your monetary undertakings in the event that you can't, while medical services mandates determine your desires for clinical therapy and delegate a chief on the off chance that you can't communicate your desires.

Systems for Resource Insurance and Move

Resource assurance systems inside home arrangements mean safeguarding your abundance from claims, lenders, and over-the-top duties. Methods, for example, the foundation of specific kinds of trusts or possession designs, can guarantee that your resources are protected and easily moved to your beneficiaries or assigned recipients. These procedures require cautious thought and frequently include lawful and monetary direction to really execute.

The Job of Life Coverage in Home Preparation

Disaster protection assumes a crucial role in home preparation, giving liquidity to your domain, covering extraordinary obligations, and being financially secure to guarantee that your friends and family. It can likewise be utilized imaginatively inside trusts to give tax-exempt advantages to your recipients, reserve magnanimous endowments, or adjust legacies among main beneficiaries, guaranteeing that your domain-arranging objectives are met in full.

Exploring Complex Family or Business Circumstances in Home Preparation

Home arranging turns out to be much more basic within the sight of perplexing relational intricacies or financial matters. Mixed families, organizations requiring progression arranging, and exceptional necessities contemplations all require custom-fit bequest arranging methodologies. These circumstances require a nuanced way to deal with guaranteeing that your resources are disseminated in a manner that lines up with your own qualities and the remarkable requirements of your recipients.

Bequest arranging is definitely not a one-time task, but a continuous interaction that develops with your life conditions. Consistently assessing and refreshing your domain plan in consultation with legal and monetary experts guarantees that it stays in line with your ongoing wishes and legitimate guidelines. By assuming command over your home preparation, you can leave an enduring, positive effect on your friends and family's lives, transforming your monetary accomplishments into a heritage that supports and improves their future.

Charge-Proficient Financial Planning

Charge-proficient financial planning is an essential methodology intended to limit charge liabilities and expand after-expense forms on ventures. It is a fundamental thought for anybody hoping to protect abundance and guarantee that their ventures keep on developing with negligible financial impedance. By getting it and using charge-productive systems, financial backers can essentially affect their drawn-out monetary achievement and dependability. This segment investigates the essentials of expense-effective financial planning and offers direction on streamlining your speculation system for charge purposes.

Essentials of Duty: Effective Financial Planning Techniques

The underpinnings of productive financial planning include

picking ventures and records that offer great expense treatment. This incorporates figuring out how different speculation salaries —like profits, interest, and capital increases—are burdened and settling on informed choices that decrease charge openness. For instance, holding ventures that create qualified profits or long-haul capital additions can offer assessment benefits over those that produce revenue pay or transient increases, which are charged at higher rates.

Using expense-advantaged records

Charge-advantaged accounts, for example, Individual Retirement Records (IRAs), 401(k)s, and Wellbeing Investment Accounts (HSAs), are essential in productive financial planning. Commitments to these records might be charge-deductible, develop charges conceded, or, on account of Roth accounts, be removed tax-exempt in retirement. Understanding the guidelines and advantages of each kind of record can assist you with choosing where to dispense your ventures to streamline charge effectiveness.

The Effect of Resource Area on Assessment Proficiency

The resource area includes decisively putting interests in accounts in view of their expense treatment to expand, generally speaking, returns. High-development or duty-wasteful resources, like specific shared assets and stocks, are appropriate for charge-advantaged accounts where their development can compound without prompt expense suggestions. On the other hand, charge-proficient ventures, as metropolitan securities, may be better positioned in available records, where they can profit from lower charge rates or exceptions.

Charge Misfortune Collecting and Its Advantages

Charge misfortune collection is a method that includes getting rid of interests at an inopportune time to balance capital increases on different ventures. This methodology can really bring down your assessment bill, permitting you to reinvest the reserve funds for future development. Consistently surveying your portfolio to recognize charge misfortune and gather valuable open doors can be a proactive method for improving duty effectiveness, particularly in unpredictable business sectors.

Contemplations for Capital Additions and Profit Pay

Overseeing ventures with an eye toward capital increases and profit pay is basic for charge proficiency. Long-haul capital gains and qualified profits commonly benefit from lower charge rates than customary pay, making them appealing to financial backers. Timing the offer of resources to fit the bill for long-haul capital increases treatment, and picking speculations that produce qualified profits can essentially lessen charge liabilities.

Charge-productive money management requires cautious preparation, progressing the board, and a profound comprehension of the duty ramifications of different ventures and records. By integrating these procedures into your speculation approach, you can shield your abundance from extreme tax assessment, guaranteeing that a greater amount of your well-deserved cash keeps on working for you over the long haul. With the right strategies, charge-effective putting can be an amazing asset in achieving independence from the rat race and saving your monetary heritage.

Retirement records and benefits

As mainstays of long-haul monetary security, retirement records and benefits are fundamental parts of an essential way to deal with abundance safeguarding. These vehicles are planned not exclusively to support people through their retirement years but also to enhance tax breaks and compound development over the long run. This part investigates the scene of retirement reserve fund choices, featuring systems to expand their true capacity and guarantee a stable monetary future.

Outline of Retirement Records

Retirement records like customary IRAs, Roth IRAs, and 401(k)s are foundational instruments for retirement reserve funds. Each type offers remarkable assessment benefits customized to various phases of a financial backer's monetary excursion. Conventional IRAs and 401(k)s give charge-conceded development; importance charges are paid upon withdrawal, and in a perfect world, at a lower charge rate in retirement. Roth IRAs, on the other hand, are supported with after-charge dollars, considering tax-exempt development and withdrawals, offering a huge benefit for those hoping to be in a higher-duty section during retirement.

Advantages of Manager-Supported Annuity Plans

Business-supported benefits plans are an important advantage, offering a characterized payout upon retirement in view of compensation and long stretches of administration. These plans, while progressively uncommon in the confidential area, turn out to have an anticipated revenue stream in retirement and frequently incorporate advantages for life partners. For those with admittance to such plans, understanding the terms and upgrading commitments can fundamentally improve retirement availability.

Methodologies for Boosting Retirement Reserve Funds

Augmenting retirement reserve funds includes something other than steady commitments; it's about essential preparation and informed direction. This incorporates making the most of manager matches in 401(k) plans, which can emphatically expand the worth of your reserve funds over the long haul. It likewise includes picking the right blend of venture choices within these records to offset development potential with risk resilience. For those with numerous retirement accounts, understanding how to designate ventures across records can streamline charging proficiency and development.

Understanding the Guidelines and Cutoff Points of Retirement Records

Exploring the complicated principles of administering retirement accounts is critical for viable retirement planning. Commitment limits, withdrawal rules, and expense suggestions shift essentially between account types. Punishments for early withdrawal and rules for required least appropriations (RMDs) require caution, wanting to stay away from superfluous expenses and punishments. Remaining informed about these guidelines guarantees that your retirement investment technique stays agreeable and proficient.

Making arrangements for conveyances and required least disseminations (RMDs)

Compelling retirement planning additionally includes planning for dissemination during retirement. This incorporates understanding the timing and duty ramifications of withdrawals from various record types. Required minimum circulations, which should start at a specific age for most retirement accounts, require cautious intention to limit charge liabilities and guarantee that your reserve funds last all through retirement. Systems, for example, Roth transformations or magnanimous gifts, can be utilized to oversee RMDs and their related assessment suggestions.

Retirement records and benefits are something beyond reserve fund vehicles; they are fundamental components of an exhaustive abundance protection methodology. By getting it and utilizing the remarkable elements of these records, people can get a monetarily stable retirement; they are persevered as well as delighted in to guarantee that their brilliant years. With smart preparation and vital administration, retirement reserve funds can provide inner harmony and monetary security, permitting retired people to receive the benefits of their long-lasting work.

Abundance Conservation Techniques

Abundance conservation is a basic part of extensive monetary preparation, pointed toward shielding the resources you've collected over your lifetime against disintegration from charges, expansion, prosecution, and different dangers. It guarantees that your abundance stays in salvageable shape to help your way of life in retirement, to give to your main beneficiaries, or to add to the causes you care about. This segment frames viable methodologies for saving your well-deserved abundance, guaranteeing it keeps on serving your objectives and values over the long haul.

Characterizing Abundance Safeguarding and Its Significance

Abundance conservation incorporates techniques intended to secure and keep up with the genuine worth of your resources. It's tied in with guaranteeing that your abundance isn't reduced by outside factors, permitting it to help your monetary objectives and accommodate people in the future. The significance of abundance protection develops as you amass resources; the more you have, the more you possibly need to lose. A proactive way to deal with abundance conservation can protect your monetary heritage and give you genuine serenity.

Putting resources into steady, long-haul resources

One essential technique for abundance safeguarding is an interest in steady, long-haul resources. These resources, for example, great securities, profit-paying stocks, and land, will generally offer consistent returns and flexibility despite market instability. Remembering these resources for your portfolio can yield a solid revenue stream and capital appreciation potential, with a lower chance of misfortune compared with additional speculative ventures.

Broadening and Chance Administration Strategies

Broadening is a vital guideline of chance administration and a foundation of abundance protection. By spreading your ventures across an assortment of resource classes, areas, geographic districts, and speculation vehicles, you can lessen the effect of any single failing to meet expectations venture on your general portfolio. Powerful expansion requires an essential methodology, considering your gamble resistance, speculation skyline, and monetary objectives to tailor a portfolio that offsets development potential with risk relief.

Legitimate Designs for Resource Assurance

Resource insurance includes legitimate methodologies to safeguard your abundance from expected leasers, claims, and decisions. Devices, for example, trusts, family-restricted organizations, and restricted obligation organizations (LLCs), can be utilized to create hindrances between your resources and likely inquirers. These designs can be perplexing and require cautious preparation and guidance from legal and monetary experts to guarantee they are laid out and worked really.

The Job of Protection in Safeguarding Abundance

Protection assumes an urgent role in abundance conservation, offering insurance against unexpected occasions that could somehow crush your monetary security. Extra security, handicap protection, long-haul care protection, and obligation protection are basic parts of a complete abundance conservation plan. Each sort of protection tends to have explicit dangers, from the deficiency of pay because of death or handicap to the expenses related to long-term care needs or lawful liabilities.

Abundance conservation is a continuous interaction that requires watchfulness, key preparation, and transformation to evolving conditions. By utilizing these systems, you can safeguard your resources from disintegration, guaranteeing they proceed to develop and serve your necessities and those of your friends and family. Powerful abundance conservation gets your monetary inheritance as well as gives the establishment a safe and prosperous future, permitting you to accomplish your drawn-out objectives and leave an enduring effect.

Magnanimous Giving and Inheritance Arranging

Magnanimous giving and inheritance arranging are significant articulations of your qualities and vision, offering a method for leaving an enduring effect on the world while likewise accomplishing charge proficiency and satisfying individual and family monetary objectives. This part investigates the coordination of charity into your monetary arrangement, specifying methodologies that benefit noble purposes as well as improving your general abundance approach.

Integrating Altruistic Surrendering into Your Monetary Arrangement

Coordinating magnanimous surrendering to your monetary and home arrangements permits you to help the causes and associations vital to you in an organized, cost-effective way. It begins with distinguishing your charitable objectives and understanding how these line up with your by-and-large monetary targets. Whether you mean to help instructive drives, clinical exploration, or human expression, a very well-created magnanimous giving system can boost the effect of your gifts while giving monetary advantages, for example, charge derivations and decreased domain charges.

Systems for Duty: An Effective Foundation

A few systems can upgrade the tax reductions of your beneficent commitments. Benefactor exhorted reserves (DAFs) permit you to make a beneficent commitment, get a prompt duty derivation, and afterward suggest awards from the asset after some time. Altruistic remaining portion trusts (CRTs) and magnanimous lead trusts (CLTs) give extra choices, offering ways of moving resources for good causes and main beneficiaries while limiting charges and possibly turning out revenue streams during your lifetime. These devices work with huge altruistic endeavors as well as coordinate these undertakings with your more extensive abundance conservation and expense-arranging techniques.

Building a Charitable Inheritance

Making a charitable inheritance includes something beyond making gifts; it's tied in with implanting your qualities into the texture of your monetary heritage. This can include laying out a confidential establishment, adding to enrichments, or taking part in effective money management. These methodologies permit you to make an organized, enduring commitment to the causes you care about, guaranteeing that your humanitarian vision goes on past your lifetime and becomes a critical part of your family's legacy.

Contemplations for Making an Enduring Effect Through Beneficent Endeavors

To have an enduring effect, it's critical to move toward beneficent giving with a similar level of vital preparation and an expected level of investment applied to different parts of your monetary life. This incorporates exploring expected beneficent beneficiaries to guarantee they line up with your qualities and objectives, understanding the best ways of supporting their work, and taking into account how to include your family in charity to impart a tradition of giving across ages.

Offsetting Altruistic Goals with Family Legacy Arranging

An exhaustive inheritance plan offsets generous objectives with the requirements and desires of your main beneficiaries. Straightforward correspondence about your magnanimous goals and the thinking behind your heritage-arranging choices can assist in adjusting family assumptions to your vision. Techniques, for example, making a family statement of purpose or including relatives in humanitarian exercises, can encourage a common obligation to beneficent giving while at the same time guaranteeing that your heritage arranging reinforces family bonds and supports your aggregate qualities.

Beneficent giving and heritage arranging are demonstrations of liberality as well as key parts of an all-encompassing monetary system. They offer a way to accomplish charge proficiency, satisfy individual qualities, and make history. By mindfully incorporating charity into your monetary preparation, you can guarantee that your abundance fills a need past private enhancement, adding to everyone's benefit and making an inheritance that mirrors your most profound responsibilities and standards.

Chapter 5: Mindset and Continuous Improvement

Fostering an Abundance Outlook

At the core of achieving independence from the rat race lies the development of an abundance outlook—aa groundbreaking way to deal with seeing and overseeing cash that recognizes the monetarily effective. This mentality isn't just about gathering abundance; it's about understanding and utilizing it to create an existence of overflow and satisfaction. This section digs into the mental groundwork of riches, offering experiences and techniques to change your outlook and embrace the rules that support monetary success.

Figuring out the mental parts of abundance

Riches, at its center, is as much about mentality as all things considered about cash. It starts with how you see abundance and what it addresses in your day-to-day existence. An abundance mentality is established in the conviction that overflow is accessible to you and that you have the influence to make and develop your abundance through your activities and choices. It includes moving past restricting convictions that view abundance as scant or unreachable, perceiving rather that with the right methodology, techniques, and devotion, monetary achievement is reachable.

Moving from a Shortage to an Overflow Mentality

The progress from a world view limited by fear, which centers around constraints and fears of not having enough, to an overflow outlook, which sees vast open doors for development and achievement, is urgent. This shift requires cognizant work to reevaluate your contemplations and convictions about cash. It includes zeroing in on potential outcomes as opposed to impediments, embracing valuable open doors for speculation and development, and having confidence in your capacity to conquer monetary difficulties.

The Significance of Defining Clear Monetary Objectives

An abundance mentality is objectively situated, underscoring the significance of setting clear, reachable monetary targets. These objectives act as a guide, directing your monetary choices and activities. Whether it's accomplishing monetary freedom, putting something aside for retirement, or building a venture portfolio, clear objectives give guidance and inspiration, assisting you with staying fixed on what you need to accomplish with your riches.

Developing Flexibility and Versatility in Monetary Issues

Flexibility and versatility are key parts of an abundance outlook. The monetary excursion is seldom straight or unsurprising; it is loaded up with promising and less promising times, triumphs, and mishaps. Developing strength implies fostering the capacity to return from monetary difficulties, while flexibility permits you to explore changing financial scenes and immediately jump all over new chances. Together, these characteristics guarantee that you stay undaunted in your quest for monetary objectives, no matter what the difficulties you face.

Conquering Mental Hindrances to Riches

Defeating mental hindrances to abundance includes distinguishing and testing firmly established convictions and fears about cash that ruin monetary advancement. This might incorporate apprehensions of disappointment, convictions about the impossibility of riches, or sensations of shamefulness. By defying these obstructions, you can start to destroy them, supplanting negative convictions with positive assertions and activities that line up with your monetary yearnings.

Fostering an abundance outlook is certainly not a short-term process; it is an excursion of self-disclosure, learning, and development. By figuring out the mental parts of riches, embracing an overflow attitude, defining clear monetary objectives, and developing flexibility and versatility, you can open the way to independence from the rat race and flourishing. This mentality is the establishment whereupon any remaining monetary techniques are constructed, directing you toward a future where abundance isn't simply a fantasy, but a reality.

The Significance of Monetary Instruction

Leaving on an excursion toward independence from the rat race is likened to heading out on the huge oceans of the monetary world. The compass directing this journey is monetary instruction—aa guide of information that enlightens the way through the intricacies of money, speculations, and abundance on the board. This section highlights the basic job of monetary training in making and supporting monetary progress, offering experiences into how ceaseless learning turns into the bedrock of a safe monetary future.

Long-Lasting Advancing as a Key to Monetary Achievement

Monetary training isn't an objective, but a ceaseless excursion of development and variation. The scene of money is steadily developing, with new items, innovations, and guidelines arising at a quick speed. Deep-rooted learning about monetary issues engages people to settle on informed choices, adjust to changes, and quickly take advantage of chances that line up with their monetary objectives. It cultivates a proactive as opposed to a receptive way to deal with individual budgets, guaranteeing that you stay in charge and directing your monetary boat with certainty and capability.

Using assets for monetary instruction

The quest for monetary information is more open than at any other time in recent memory because of the abundance of assets readily available. Books, online courses, webcasts, and monetary websites offer a gold mine of data, taking special care of each and every degree of monetary skill. Drawing in with these assets can extend how you might interpret monetary standards, venture techniques, and monetary patterns, giving you the devices you really want to explore the monetary world with affirmation.

Remaining Refreshed with Monetary News and Patterns

Staying up-to-date with monetary news and patterns is critical for informed, independent direction. The worldwide economy, securities exchanges, loan costs, and monetary approaches straightforwardly influence individual accounting and speculation potential opening doors. By remaining informed, you can expect market developments, change your monetary methodologies appropriately, and shield your resources from possible slumps. This carefulness guarantees that your monetary plans stay in line with the more extensive financial climate, improving your capacity to profit by patterns and alleviating chances.

Gaining from Monetary Errors and Victories

Monetary instruction additionally includes thoughtfulness—gaining from your own monetary mix-ups and triumphs. Thinking about past monetary choices, understanding what turned out badly or right, and drawing examples from these encounters are important for self-awareness. This intelligent practice develops monetary insight, empowering you to refine your techniques, keep away from rehash blunders, and repeat triumphs, consequently propelling your monetary keenness and strength.

Drawing in with the Monetary People Group for Information Sharing

Cooperation in monetary networks, whether online gatherings, venture clubs, or instructive studios, offers the chance for information sharing and joint effort. Drawing in with companions and specialists in these settings can provide different viewpoints, pragmatic guidance, and backing, enhancing your monetary training venture. These people encourage an aggregate learning climate where bits of knowledge, encounters, and techniques are unreservedly traded, adding to your monetary proficiency and strengthening it.

The significance of monetary training in the journey for independence from the rat race couldn't possibly be more significant. It is the establishment whereupon informed choices are made, gambles are made, and amazing open doors are seized. By focusing on deep-rooted getting the hang of, remaining educated, thinking about encounters, and drawing in with monetary networks, you can explore the intricacies of individual accounting with certainty. This obligation to monetary schooling prepares for enduring achievement, guaranteeing that you are exceptional to accomplish your monetary yearnings and secure your monetary future.

Adjusting to Monetary Change

The monetary scene is all around as powerful as the seasons, continually developing with shifts in financial circumstances, market patterns, and individual life-altering situations. The capacity to adjust to these progressions is a sign of monetary sharpness and a critical determinant of long-haul monetary dependability and development. This section investigates the significance of adaptability in monetary preparation, offering techniques to explore through times of progress and vulnerability with dexterity and premonition.

Perceiving and Answering Monetary Movements

Monetary cycles and market changes are unavoidable, affecting venture returns, work opportunities, and in general monetary prosperity. Perceiving these movements as they happen and understanding their likely effect on your funds is pivotal. Adjusting to monetary changes might include changing your venture portfolio to alleviate risk, modifying your ways of managing money to save capital, or investigating new pay opportunities because of the gig market's requests. The capacity to quickly answer financial movements shields your resources as well as positions you to gain from the open doors that emerge during monetary recuperations.

Embracing Innovation and Development in Money

The computerized economy has changed the monetary area, presenting plenty of devices and stages that have improved control over individual budgets and speculations. Embracing innovation and advancement in finance, from web-based banking and speculation applications to fintech answers for planning and abundance across the board, can altogether improve your capacity to oversee and develop your riches. These devices provide constant information, logical experiences, and smoothed-out processes, enabling you to make informed choices quickly and effectively.

Exploring Individual Life-Altering Events with Monetary Ramifications

Life's achievements—marriage, being a parent, profession changes, and retirement—have huge monetary ramifications. Adjusting your monetary arrangement to line up with these life-altering events is fundamental. This might include reconsidering your spending plan, refreshing your protection inclusion, changing your reserve fund objectives, or rethinking your speculation system. Expecting and anticipating these occasions guarantees that your monetary arrangement stays applicable and powerful, fit for supporting your developing requirements and goals.

Changing Monetary Methodologies to Keep Up with Progress

As you venture through life's monetary scene, occasional audits and acclimations to your monetary methodology are basic. This proactive methodology permits you to remain focused on your monetary objectives, making vital course revisions because of both outside changes and changes in your own monetary circumstances. Whether it's rebalancing your venture portfolio, reexamining your retirement reserve fund plan, or redistributing assets to address new needs, adaptability in your monetary procedure is critical to keeping up with progress and making long-term progress.

The Job of Adaptability in Monetary Preparation

Adaptability in monetary arranging isn't about consistent change; it's about keeping up with the harmony between immovability in your objectives and versatility in your methodology. It's tied in with having the strength to endure monetary tempests and the deftness to move with the flows of progress. By embracing an adaptable mentality, you equip yourself with the ability to explore through vulnerability, jump all over arising chances, and steer your monetary future toward success and security.

Adjusting to monetary change is a vital ability to chase after independence from the rat race. It requires cautiousness, the availability to embrace new advances, and the capacity to change your monetary plans in light of life's unavoidable movements. With versatility as a core value, you can unhesitatingly confront the back and forth movements of the monetary world, transforming difficulties into venturing stones toward accomplishing your monetary dreams.

Building an encouraging group of people

The excursion toward independence from the rat race, similar to any critical campaign, is best explored fully supported by proficient and dependable buddies. Building an encouraging group of people—coaches, counselors, and similar companions—can give you direction, support, and significant experiences as you diagram your course through the intricacies of individual budgets. This section stresses the basic job of an encouraging group of people in making monetary progress, framing how to develop and use these connections to improve your monetary excursion.

The Worth of Tutors, Counsels, and Monetary Experts

Tutors and monetary counselors offer an abundance of involvement and information on real value, offering customized direction custom-made to your novel monetary circumstances and objectives. A guide who has effectively explored their own monetary excursion can offer functional exhortation, examples learned, and systems that have demonstrated success. Proficient monetary counselors, outfitted with specialized aptitude in monetary preparation, ventures, and assessment techniques, can give you particular direction to enhance your monetary choices. Drawing in with these experts can speed up your headway, assist you in keeping away from normal traps and settling on informed decisions that line up with your drawn-out goals.

Utilizing People Group Assets and Care Groups

Networks, both on the web and disconnected, act as lively environments for information trade and backing. Taking part in monetary studios, workshops, and gatherings offers amazing chances to gain from specialists and friends alike. Online people groups and web-based entertainment bunches zeroed in on individual accounting and contributing can be significant assets, offering admittance to a different scope of points of view, encounters, and counsel. Participating in these networks supports consistent learning and keeps you informed about the most recent monetary devices, patterns, and systems.

The Effect of Companion Backing on Monetary Direction

Peer support assumes a huge part in monetary navigation, offering both moral help and viable guidance. Loved ones who share your monetary desires or who have left on comparable monetary excursions can give support, responsibility, and a feeling of brotherhood. Sharing encounters, difficulties, and triumphs with friends can offer new experiences, spur you to keep on track, and celebrate achievements together, supporting your obligation to your monetary objectives.

Making Responsible Associations for Monetary Objectives

Responsibility organizations are an amazing asset for keeping up with concentration and energy toward accomplishing your monetary goals. Bringing together with somebody who considers you responsible for your monetary plans and objectives can essentially expand your odds of coming out on top. These associations include customary registrations, sharing advancement, laying out common objectives, and giving helpful input. A responsibility accomplice persuades you to persist as well as fills in as a sounding board for thoughts and methodologies, improving your dynamic cycle.

Organizing for potential open doors and experiences

Organizing with experts and friends in the monetary business can open new doors, experiences, and joint efforts. Building associations with people across different areas can expand how you might interpret the monetary scene, acquaint you with speculation, open valuable doors, and associate you with assets and experts who can aid your monetary excursion. Organizing is tied in with making commonly valuable connections, where the trading of information, encounters, and backing cultivates development and a chance for all included.

Building an encouraging group of people is a fundamental part of fruitful monetary preparation and establishing a strong financial foundation. By encircling yourself with guides, counselors, friends, and responsibility accomplices who share your monetary vision and values, you create an underpinning of help that impels you toward your objectives. This organization gives direction and understanding as well as rouses certainty, inspiration, and flexibility, guaranteeing that your way to independence from the rat race is both informed and improved by the aggregate insight and experience of people around you.

Deep-rooted Monetary Procedures

The mission for independence from the rat race isn't a run, but a long-distance race, requesting quick activity as well as supported exertion and devotion. Deep-rooted monetary methodologies are the diagram for this perseverance through venture, exemplifying rules that guide you through different phases of life and adjusting as conditions advance. This section distils the substance of making and keeping a monetary arrangement that endures everyday hardship as well as twists, guaranteeing a tradition of riches and insight for a long time into the future.

Laying out Propensities for Long-Haul Monetary Wellbeing

The groundwork for long-lasting monetary achievement is based on everyday propensities that, over the long run, compound into significant abundance. These propensities incorporate restrained saving, judicious spending, ordinary money management, and consistent learning. Like the consistent dribble of water that ultimately fills a pail, reliable use of these propensities can change unassuming endeavors into a critical monetary repository. Developing these propensities requires care and responsibility, making way for a future where monetary security and opportunity are goals as well as real factors.

Routinely checking on and changing monetary plans

A monetary arrangement is a living report, one that mirrors what is happening, objectives, and methodologies. As life unfolds, your monetary arrangement should advance, obliging new objectives, evolving conditions, and surprising difficulties. Normal audits—to some extent every year or after significant life-altering situations—guarantee that your arrangement stays in line with your drawn-out targets. These audits offer chances to rethink your venture portfolio, change your reserve fund systems, and refine your monetary objectives, guaranteeing that your arrangement stays responsive and important.

Consolidating new monetary items and procedures

The monetary scene is dynamic, with new items, devices, and procedures arising consistently. Remaining educated and open to integrating these advancements can upgrade your monetary arrangement's viability. Whether it's utilizing robo-counselors for venture executives, investigating elective speculations for broadening, or using fintech answers for planning and saving, new monetary items can offer chances to advance your monetary systems, further develop productivity, and possibly increment returns.

Planning for Future Monetary Difficulties and Valuable Open Doors

Expecting future monetary difficulties and valuable open doors is a basic part of long-lasting monetary preparation. This prescience includes not simply defending against expected gambles—like market unpredictability, financial slumps, or individual crises—but additionally situating yourself to gain by opening doors. Building a backup stash, keeping a differentiated speculation portfolio, and consistently extending your monetary information prepare you to explore future vulnerabilities with certainty, transforming likely obstructions into venturing stones towards your monetary objectives.

Obligation to Individual and Monetary Development

At the core of deep-rooted monetary methodologies lies a guarantee of individual and monetary development. This responsibility implies effectively looking for valuable chances to grow your insight, abilities, and comprehension of the individual budget and abundance of executives. It includes embracing difficulties as growth opportunities, commending triumphs as achievements, and surveying mishaps as any open doors for development. By focusing on nonstop improvement and variation, you guarantee that your monetary excursion isn't just about arriving at an objective; it's about developing, learning, and flourishing enroute.

Deep-rooted monetary methodologies are the foundation for persevering through independence from the rat race and achievement. By laying out sound monetary propensities, consistently exploring and changing your monetary arrangement, consolidating new monetary items, planning for future difficulties, and focusing on continuous development, you lay the foundation for a monetary heritage described by shrewdness, security, and flourishing. This all-encompassing methodology guarantees that your monetary excursion is stamped by the abundance you gather as well as by the monetary sharpness and versatility you create, offering significant examples for generations to follow.

Conclusion

As we arrive at the end of our excursion through "The Abundance Outline: Methodologies for Independence from the Rat Race," it is fundamental to ponder the center standards and techniques that have been the bedrock of our investigation. This restatement serves not just as a sign of what we have realized but additionally as a reference point to direct us forward as we continue looking for monetary freedom.

Rundown of Fundamental Monetary Systems Canvassed in the Book

We started by laying the groundwork for planning and the basic significance of figuring out your monetary inflow and surge. The production of a spending plan that works for you is the most important phase in assuming command over your monetary predetermination. From that point, we dove into the meaning of saving and building a backup stash, guaranteeing you are ready for life's capricious minutes without crashing your monetary plans.

Contributing arose as a critical subject, with conversations on differentiating pay through stocks, securities, common assets, ETFs, land, and even digital forms of money. Every speculation vehicle was investigated inside and out, furnishing you with the information to settle on informed choices that line up with your gamble resilience and monetary objectives.

Bequest arranging, proficient money management, and the use of retirement accounts highlighted the significance of anticipating the future, both for you and for a long time into the future. These parts highlighted the need for proactive measures to safeguard and develop your abundance over the long haul.

Featuring the Significance of Planning, Saving, Money Management, and Arranging

Planning, saving, effective money management, and arranging structure are the mainstays of independence from the rat race. Every part assumes a pivotal role in building a safe monetary future. Planning gives lucidity and command over your funds; saving sets you up for the unforeseen; contributing offers the potential for abundance and development; and arranging guarantees that your monetary objectives are met with prescience and accuracy.

Emphasizing the Job of Outlook in Accomplishing Independence from the Rat Race

Vital to the whole plan is the idea of outlook. Fostering an abundance outlook—aa blend of assurance, energy, and faith in overflow—is key to changing your monetary reality. This outlook supports flexibility even with difficulties and encourages a persistent quest for information and development.

In summing up these key systems, we are helped to remember the complete idea of independence from the rat race. It isn't accomplished through a solitary activity, but through a steady, comprehensive methodology that encompasses each part of the individual budget. As you push ahead, let these standards guide your choices, activities, and mentalities towards cash. Keep in mind that independence from the rat race isn't just an objective, but rather an excursion—one that is as much about self-awareness as it's worth about monetary development.

Making a move: following stages

With the basic information on "The Abundance Outline: Systems for Independence from the Rat Race" readily available, the subsequent stage is clear: activity. Changing monetary information into unmistakable outcomes requires purposeful advances, responsibility, and an essential methodology. This section expects to direct you from understanding to execution, illustrating a way ahead that turns an interpretation of experiences into results.

Directions on Executing the Techniques Talked About

The excursion towards independence from the rat race starts with a far-reaching survey of your ongoing monetary circumstances. Survey your pay, costs, obligations, and reserve funds with a basic eye, utilizing the techniques examined as a structure for development. Make a point-by-point plan that includes location planning, crisis reserve funds, obligation reimbursement, and speculation objectives, custom-fitting to your remarkable conditions and goals.

It is vital to define noteworthy objectives. Characterize clear, quantifiable targets with explicit timetables. Whether it's saving a specific sum in something like a year, taking care of obligations within a particular period, or accomplishing a designated speculation return, these objectives ought to act as achievements on your way to monetary freedom.

Putting forth Noteworthy Objectives and Making a Course of Events

Your monetary arrangement ought to incorporate present-moment, medium-term, and long-term objectives, each joined by a practical course of events. Momentary objectives could zero in on quick enhancements in planning and saving; medium-term objectives could focus on obligation decrease and venture systems; and long-haul objectives probably revolve around retirement planning and abundance amassing. Focus on these objectives in light of their desperation and significance, designating your assets appropriately.

Consolation to Venture Out Towards Monetary Autonomy

Venturing out can frequently be the most difficult aspect of any excursion. It expects fortitude to stand up to real monetary factors and the assurance to transform them. Keep in mind that each critical accomplishment starts with the choice to attempt. Begin a little on the off chance that you really want to—maybe by making a spending plan, opening a bank account, or instructing yourself on speculation choices. The key is to start.

The change from wanting to activity is a basic stage in your monetary excursion. It requests discipline, steadiness, and the readiness to adjust as conditions change. Focus on your objectives; however, be adaptable in your strategies, changing your arrangement as you learn and develop. Praise every accomplishment, regardless of how little, and gain from each difficulty.

In making these next strides, you're not simply moving towards independence from the rat race; you're embracing a way of life of proactive monetary administration. This approach is certainly not a transitory fix, but rather a long-lasting obligation to accomplishing and keeping up with monetary prosperity. Allow this section to act as both a source of inspiration and an aide, empowering you to apply the information acquired with certainty and clarity. The way to monetary autonomy is yours to walk, and an opportunity to venture out is currently there.

Remaining Inspired

Setting out on the excursion toward independence from the rat race is an undertaking loaded with difficulties and wins. It requires not just a strong arrangement and the right techniques, but also a supported inspiration to continue to push forward, in any event, when obstructions emerge. Remaining persuaded on this excursion is fundamental, as it powers your responsibility and drives you to accomplish your monetary objectives. This part is devoted to sustaining that inspiration, giving systems to keep up with your energy and resolve, and guaranteeing you stay on the way to monetary achievement.

Systems for Keeping Up with Inspiration on the Excursion to Independence from the Rat Race

The way to monetary autonomy is defaced with expected

misfortunes and slow advancement. To keep your spirits high, set more modest, attainable achievements within your bigger objectives. These go about as designated spots, providing you with a feeling of achievement and an unmistakable proportion of progress. Praising these achievements, whether it's taking care of a charge card, arriving at a reserve fund target, or making your most memorable speculation, builds up a certain way of behaving and keeps you persuaded.

The Significance of Observing Achievements and Gaining from Mishaps

Festivity is a strong inspiration. It helps you remember why you began this excursion and what you're pursuing. Alternately, misfortunes are unavoidable, but not inconceivable. Seeing them as learning amazing things opens doors instead of disappointments, which is urgent. Dissect what turned out badly, change your arrangement as needed, and push ahead with recharged assurance. This versatile outlook transforms difficulties into stepping stones, not hindrances.

Building an encouraging group of people for support and responsibility

No excursion ought to be embraced alone, and the way to independence from the rat race is no exception. Encircling yourself with a steady organization of family, companions, and monetary guides who offer or support your objectives can provide consolation, counsel, and responsibility. Imparting your objectives to this organization frees you up to important criticism as well as a feeling of responsibility, making you bound to see everything through to completion. Moreover, consider joining monetary gatherings or web-based entertainment groups where you can track down motivation and support those in comparable ways.

Remaining roused Chasing monetary freedom isn't exclusively about praising victories or exploring difficulties; it's additionally about constantly helping yourself to remember the bigger vision.

Return to your monetary objectives routinely, helping yourself to remember the opportunity and security you're pursuing. Envision the way of life you're intending to accomplish, the inner harmony that accompanies monetary security, and the delight of arriving at your objectives. This perception fills in as a strong sign of your "why," keeping your inspiration lit.

Embracing the Excursion

At last, comprehend that the excursion to independence from the rat race is as much about self-improvement as, for all intents and purposes, monetary development. Each step, whether forward or reverse, shows you something significant about yourself, your relationship with cash, and how you handle difficulties. Embrace this excursion with an open heart and brain, prepared to learn, adjust, and develop. The quest for independence from the rat race isn't just about the objective; it's about turning out to be all the more monetarily insightful, versatile, and enabled enroute.

Keeping up with inspiration is basic to achieving independence from the rat race. It pushes you forward, supports you through difficulties, and makes your objectives reachable. By commending achievements, gaining from misfortunes, fabricating a steady organization, and embracing the excursion, you can maintain an elevated degree of inspiration that will direct you to monetary achievement. Keep in mind that the way to independence from the rat race is a long-distance race, not a run; remaining roused is critical to crossing the end goal.

Assets for Additional Learning

The way to independence from the rat race is through consistent training and development. As the monetary scene advances, so too should your insights and methodologies. This obligation to deep-rooted learning is fundamental for keeping up with and improving your monetary prosperity. This section gives a guide to assets that can develop your comprehension, hone your monetary discernment, and keep you educated regarding the most recent patterns and developments in individual budgets.

Suggested Books, Sites, and Courses for Proceeding with Monetary Instruction

The excursion of monetary schooling is extraordinarily improved by a great many assets. Books created by monetary specialists offer top-to-bottom bits of knowledge into individual accounting, effective financial planning, abundance on the board, and the mental parts of cash. Sites and online stages give exceptional data on market patterns, venture valuable open doors, and monetary news, while online courses offer organized learning ways on unambiguous themes, from fundamental planning to cutting-edge money management techniques. Enhancing your wellsprings of data guarantees a balanced comprehension and keeps you connected with and informed.

Drawing in with the Monetary People Group and Expert Exhortation

Monetary groups, both on the web and in reality, offer significant open doors for learning and development. Gatherings, virtual entertainment gatherings, and speculation clubs can offer help, answer questions, and deal with assorted points of view on monetary difficulties and potential open doors. Besides, talking with monetary counselors or experts can give customized exhortations tailored to your special monetary circumstances and objectives. These specialists can offer direction on complex issues, assist you with exploring monetary choices, and give you responsibility.

Featuring the Significance of Remaining Refreshed with Monetary News and Patterns

The monetary world is dynamic, with new turns of events, strategies, and advancements arising consistently. Remaining informed about these progressions is pivotal for adjusting your monetary methodologies to keep up with and develop your riches. Routinely perusing monetary news, buying into monetary pamphlets, and following legitimate monetary experts and pundits can assist you with remaining in front of patterns and pursuing informed choices.

In a period where data is plentiful, the test frequently lies in knowing its quality and importance. Focus on assets that are respectable, proof-based, and line up with your monetary qualities and objectives. Keep in mind that the objective of drawing in with these assets isn't simply to aggregate information but to apply this information to settle on better monetary choices.

The deep-rooted student's benefit in an individual budget

The best people in individual accounting are those who focus on being long-lasting students. They comprehend that monetary instruction is definitely not a one-time occasion but rather a persistent interaction. By reliably searching out new information, remaining inquisitive about the monetary world, and being available to have a significant impact on points of view, you can adjust to the steadily changing monetary scene. This approach not only upgrades your capacity to accomplish independence from the rat race, but in addition improves your existence with a more profound comprehension of how to successfully oversee and develop your riches.

Assets for additional learning are your apparatuses and partners on the excursion to independence from the rat race. They enable you to fabricate a strong groundwork of information, remain light-footed in an impactful world, and settle on choices that line up with your objectives and values. Embrace these assets with a promise to development, and you will wind up exceptional enough to explore the way to monetary achievement and then some.

Separating inspirational statements

As we close the last pages of "The Abundance Plan: Systems for Independence from the Rat Race," it's vital to perceive that the excursion you're leaving on is one of significant change and strengthening. The way to independence from the rat race is set apart by difficulties and triumphs, questions and revelations, or, more importantly, development. These uplifting statements are intended to act as an encouraging sign and motivation as you explore your monetary excursion.

Rousing Last Contemplations to Spur Perusers

Keep in mind that independence from the rat race isn't exclusively about amassing abundance; it's about what that abundance empowers you to do. The opportunity to pursue decisions that line up with your qualities, the capacity to accommodate your friends and family, and the valuable chance to leave an enduring effect on the world. The excursion to independence from the rat race is as much about the individual you become as, for all intents and purposes, about the resources you aggregate.

Reaffirming Confidence in the Peruser's Capacity to Accomplish Independence from the Rat Race

You have inside you all that you require to accomplish independence from the rat race. The procedures, bits of knowledge, and standards framed in this book are apparatuses available to you, yet your most prominent resource is your obligation to your monetary prosperity. Have confidence in yourself and your capacity to make educated, trained monetary choices. With determination, versatility, and an eagerness to learn, you can and will arrive at your monetary objectives.

Underscoring the Excursion's Worth and the Extraordinary Force of Monetary Freedom

The worth of your excursion to independence from the rat race lies in the objective as well as in the examples advanced enroute. Each forward-moving step, regardless of how little, is progress. Embrace the cycle, knowing that with each challenge you survive, you're nearer to your monetary objectives as well as turning out to be more capable, certain, and monetarily sharp.

Monetary freedom is groundbreaking. It offers security and inner harmony as well as the opportunity to seek after your interests, investigate new open doors, and settle on decisions that advance your life and the existence of people around you. The way might be long and, on occasion, troublesome; however, the prizes—both monetary and individual—are vast.

As you push ahead, outfitted with the information and procedures from this book, recall that you are in good company. There is a local area of people in comparative ways, and there are assets accessible to guide and support you. Remain inquisitive, remain inspired, and, in particular, stick with it. Your independence from the rat race venture is one of the most rewarding ventures you will at any point embrace.

Let these splitting inspirational statements be a consistent update that your desires for independence from the rat race are substantial, reachable, and deserving of pursuit. With each step you take, realize that you're making progress toward monetary freedom as well as creating a tradition of shrewdness, versatility, and strengthening for you and others in the future. Continue to push forward, for the excursion is all around as rewarding as the objective.